this journal
BELONGS TO

A TRIBUTE TO A LEGEND

Born March 15, 1933, in Brooklyn, New York, Ruth Bader Ginsburg was the second woman appointed to the Supreme Court of the United States. Ginsburg graduated from Cornell University, attended Harvard Law School, and graduated from Columbia Law School at the top of her class. Despite her phenomenal academic achievements, Ginsburg faced challenges finding a job because of her gender, but she persisted in establishing a renowned legal career as an attorney and professor. She was a pioneering champion for democracy, women, and voting rights and served as associate justice of the Supreme Court from 1993 until her death in 2020. Known for her powerful legal mind and dissenting opinions, Ginsburg devoted her career to fighting for women's rights as a constitutional principle. In 2002, she was inducted into the National Women's Hall of Fame, was named one of *Forbes* magazine's 100 Most Powerful Women from 2004 through 2011, and in 2015, *Time* magazine included her as one of the Time 100. In addition to the countless legal landmarks she made possible, Ginsburg became a cultural and feminist icon with nearly rock-star status toward the end of her storied life, representing hope and inspiration for empowered women everywhere. This journal is dedicated to the life and legacy of Ruth Bader Ginsburg.

"**FIGHT** FOR THE THINGS THAT YOU CARE ABOUT, BUT DO IT IN A WAY THAT WILL **LEAD** OTHERS TO JOIN YOU."

—RUTH BADER GINSBURG

"WOMEN BELONG
IN ALL PLACES
WHERE DECISIONS
ARE BEING MADE."

—RUTH BADER GINSBURG

"I ASK NO FAVOR
        FOR MY SEX.
ALL I ASK OF OUR BRETHREN
IS THAT THEY
        TAKE THEIR FEET
OFF OUR NECKS."

—RUTH BADER GINSBURG

"SO OFTEN IN LIFE,
THINGS THAT YOU REGARD
AS AN IMPEDIMENT
TURN OUT TO BE GREAT,
GOOD FORTUNE."

—RUTH BADER GINSBURG

"WOMEN WILL HAVE ACHIEVED TRUE EQUALITY WHEN MEN SHARE WITH THEM THE RESPONSIBILITY OF BRINGING UP THE NEXT GENERATION."

—RUTH BADER GINSBURG

"I DISSENT."

—RUTH BADER GINSBURG

"YET WHAT GREATER
DEFEAT COULD WE SUFFER
THAN TO COME TO RESEMBLE
THE FORCES WE OPPOSE
IN THEIR DISRESPECT FOR
HUMAN DIGNITY?"

—RUTH BADER GINSBURG

"PEOPLE ASK ME SOMETIMES, 'WHEN—WHEN DO YOU THINK IT WILL BE ENOUGH? WHEN WILL THERE BE ENOUGH WOMEN ON THE COURT?' AND MY ANSWER IS WHEN THERE ARE NINE."

—RUTH BADER GINSBURG

"IT IS NOT
WOMEN'S LIBERATION,
IT IS WOMEN'S
AND
MEN'S LIBERATION."

—RUTH BADER GINSBURG

"MY MOTHER TOLD ME
TO BE A LADY. AND
FOR HER, THAT MEANT
BE YOUR OWN PERSON,
BE INDEPENDENT."

—RUTH BADER GINSBURG

"AS WOMEN ACHIEVE POWER,
THE BARRIERS WILL FALL.
AS SOCIETY SEES
WHAT WOMEN CAN DO,
AS WOMEN SEE WHAT
WOMEN CAN DO,
THERE WILL BE MORE
WOMEN OUT THERE DOING
THINGS, AND WE'LL ALL BE
BETTER OFF FOR IT."

—RUTH BADER GINSBURG

"THAT'S THE
     DISSENTER'S HOPE:
THAT THEY ARE WRITING
NOT FOR TODAY,
     BUT FOR TOMORROW."

—RUTH BADER GINSBURG

"I'VE GOTTEN MUCH MORE
SATISFACTION FOR THE
THINGS THAT I'VE DONE FOR
WHICH I WAS NOT PAID."

—RUTH BADER GINSBURG

"IF YOU WANT TO BE
A TRUE PROFESSIONAL,
YOU WILL DO SOMETHING
OUTSIDE YOURSELF...
SOMETHING THAT MAKES
LIFE A LITTLE BETTER
FOR PEOPLE LESS FORTUNATE
THAN YOU."

—RUTH BADER GINSBURG

This publication is designed to provide accurate and authoritative information in regard to the subject matter covered. It is sold with the understanding that the publisher is not engaged in rendering legal, accounting, or other professional service. If legal advice or other expert assistance is required, the services of a competent professional person should be sought.
—From a Declaration of Principles Jointly Adopted by a Committee of the American Bar Association and a Committee of Publishers and Associations

Published by Sourcebooks
P.O. Box 4410, Naperville, Illinois 60567-4410
(630) 961-3900
sourcebooks.com

Printed and bound in the United States of America.
VP 10 9 8 7 6 5 4 3 2